John Smith:

Explorer and Colonial Leader

Explorers of New Worlds

Vasco Núñez de Balboa and the Discovery of the South Sea

Daniel Boone and the Exploration of the Frontier

John Cabot and the Rediscovery of North America

Jacques Cartier and the Exploration of Canada

Christopher Columbus and the Discovery of the New World

James Cook and the Exploration of the Pacific

Francisco Coronado and the Exploration of the American Southwest

Hernando Cortés and the Conquest of Mexico

Jacques Cousteau and the Undersea World

Sir Francis Drake and the Foundation of a World Empire

John C. Frémont: Pathfinder of the West

Vasco da Gama and the Portuguese Explorers

Sir Edmund Hillary: Modern-Day Explorer

Henry Hudson: Ill-Fated Explorer of North America's Coast

Jolliet and Marquette: Explorers of the Mississippi River

La Salle and the Exploration of the Mississippi

Lewis and Clark: Explorers of the Louisiana Purchase

Ferdinand Magellan and the First Voyage Around the World

Robert Peary and the Quest for the North Pole

Francisco Pizarro and the Conquest of the Inca

Marco Polo and the Wonders of the East

Juan Ponce de León and the Search for the Fountain of Youth

Sir Walter Raleigh and the Search for El Dorado

Reaching for the Moon: The Apollo Astronauts

Theodore Roosevelt and the Exploration of the Amazon Basin

Sacagawea: Guide for the Lewis and Clark Expedition

Sir Ernest Shackleton and the Struggle Against Antarctica

John Smith: Explorer and Colonial Leader

Hernando de Soto and the Exploration of Florida

The Viking Explorers

John Smith:

Explorer and Colonial Leader

Hal Marcovitz

Chelsea House Publishers
Philadelphia

Prepared for Chelsea House Publishers by:
OTTN Publishing, Stockton, N.J.

CHELSEA HOUSE PUBLISHERS
Editor in Chief: Sally Cheney
Associate Editor in Chief: Kim Shinners
Production Manager: Pamela Loos
Art Director: Sara Davis
Director of Photography: Judy L. Hasday
Project Editors: LeeAnne Gelletly, Brian Baughan
Series Designer: Keith Trego

3 5 7 9 8 6 4 2

Library of Congress Cataloging-in-Publication Data

Marcovitz, Hal.
    John Smith, explorer and colonial leader / Hal
    Marcovitz.
        p. cm.–(Explorers of new worlds)
Includes bibliographical references and index.
ISBN 0-7910-6432-8 (alk. paper)
1. Smith, John, 1580–1631–Juvenile literature.
2. Colonists–Virginia–Jamestown–Biography–Juvenile
literature. 3. Explorers–America–Biography–Juvenile
literature. 4. Explorers–England–Biography–Juvenile
literature. 5. Jamestown (Va.)–History–17th century–
Juvenile literature. 6. Jamestown (Va.)–Biography–
Juvenile literature. 7. Virginia–History–Colonial period,
ca. 1600-1775–Juvenile literature. I. Title. II. Series.

F229.S7 M37 2001
973.2'1'092–dc21
    [B]   2001028203

Contents

"Two Great Stones"

Pocahontas throws herself across the body of John Smith, saving the English explorer from being killed by her father's warriors. This is the traditional story, told by Smith in one of his books; the actual facts of the event are uncertain, but may have been quite different.

I

The Indians caught up with Captain John Smith and his companions along the Chickahominy River, just west of the settlement at Jamestown. Smith and some soldiers from the settlement had been on a hunting *expedition*. The settlers at Jamestown had little food, and it was Smith's job to keep people from going hungry.

While searching for food in the Virginia wilderness, Smith and the soldiers had to be wary of the Algonquian

Indians, who at times were hostile. This time, Smith and his men were caught off guard. Two soldiers died in the **skirmish**, and Smith and the others were taken prisoner. The Englishmen were taken to the village of the Algonquian chief, Powhatan.

Nearly 400 years have passed since Captain John Smith met Powhatan. What happened during this famous encounter has become part of American folklore. Told and retold hundreds of times over the years, the story that most people learn today has clearly strayed from the truth. This is not surprising, since Captain Smith often took many liberties with the facts when it suited his purpose.

Smith was an explorer, mapmaker, geographer, soldier, politician, merchant, sailor, and writer. He was also a proud and boastful man. He lived through many adventures in his life, and he was not above blurring the lines between truth and fiction in his accounts of those adventures.

Still, no one doubts that in the winter of 1607, John Smith met up with the Algonquian chief Powhatan. Smith had been in tight places before and had always managed to escape, either through his cleverness or, if necessary, his skill with the sword. Indeed, during his 29 years Smith had fought

This 1622 map of Virginia, drawn with John Smith's help, shows Chief Powhatan in the upper left corner.

in combat, sailed with pirates, and escaped from slavery. Just a few weeks before his capture by the Algonquians, he had been captured by another tribe. During that episode, the captain managed to trade his freedom for the compass in his pocket.

Smith believed he was in more danger from the Algonquians. He feared Powhatan was trying to rid his land of the settlers.

There are four versions of how Smith managed to escape his captors.

The first version was written by Smith in his 1608 book, which he gave the rather unwieldy title of "A True Relation of Such Occurrences and Accidents of Note as hath Happened in Virginia since the First Planning of that Colony."

According to Smith, he persuaded Powhatan to send a message back to Jamestown reporting that he was alive and well and would rejoin the settlement soon. Smith wrote the note, and Powhatan entrusted it to three braves, who carried it to the settlement. However, instead of reporting that Smith was safe, the note really said that the settlement should make ready for an attack by the hostile Algonquians. After delivering the message, the three braves turned to go back to Powhatan's camp. Behind them, the settlers unleashed a volley of *musket* fire from the fort. This frightened the messengers, who returned

When others wrote about their experiences in the New World, many questioned the truthfulness of Smith's books. George Percy, an original Jamestown settler, wrote that the captain's book was stuffed with "many falsities and malicious detractions."

to camp and told Powhatan the tale of the awesome firepower in the fort. After hearing this report, Powhatan released Smith.

But in 1617, Smith updated his book with a much different story. In this version, Smith was brought before Powhatan, who demanded to know what Smith was doing in his territory. Powhatan, Smith related, suspected him of planning to make war on the Algonquians. Unsatisfied with Smith's answer that the party from Jamestown was simply looking for food, the chief condemned the captain to death.

"Two great stones were brought before Powhatan," the captain wrote. "Then, as many as could laid hands on [Smith], dragged him to them, and thereon laid his head, and being ready with their clubs, to beat out his brains."

What Smith claimed happened next is the subject of much dispute. Nevertheless, it is an American legend. According to Smith, Powhatan's young daughter Pocahontas stepped forward and pleaded with her father to save the captain's life.

Then, Smith wrote, Powhatan's heart softened—the chief could never refuse a plea by his favorite daughter—and he ordered Smith released. In fact, Smith wrote, Powhatan not only let him go, but he gave him land, made him a member of the tribe, and treated him as a son. Smith stayed among the Indians for a few more days, then returned to Jamestown.

It is likely that Smith came up with that story because in 1617, Pocahontas had arrived in England with her new husband, Virginia tobacco grower John Rolfe. The Indian princess was the talk of London; she had been introduced to the royal court, where King James and Queen Anne had grown fond of her. Certainly, Smith may have conjured up that story as a way to share in some of her celebrity.

Later, Smith would come up with yet another version of his meeting with Powhatan. This time, Smith wrote, he bought his freedom by agreeing to give Powhatan two cannons and a *millstone*. When Smith returned to Jamestown to fulfill the bargain, the settlers gave the Indians the cannons but filled them with rocks, rendering them useless.

Over the years, historians have studied those three stories and have come up with a fourth version. They believe that when Powhatan ordered two stones brought before the captain, the Indian leader intended to use the stones as an *initiation* rite. Perhaps the Algonquians were not as hostile as Smith

Pocahontas was about 12 years old in the winter of 1607. Although Smith hinted in his book that he had been romantically involved with her, this is an obvious tall tale. Pocahontas eventually married John Rolfe and moved to England, where this portrait was painted.

Matoaks als Rebecka daughter to the mighty Prince Powhatan Emperour of Attanoughkomouck als Virginia converted and baptized in the Christian faith, and Wife to the wor: Mr Tho: Rolff.

wanted his readers to think, and they intended to welcome him to the tribe as a new brother. It is possible that the captain misunderstood the meaning of the stones and thought his life was in danger.

Clearly, though, the story of Pocahontas has endured and become part of the story of America. In fact, a visitor to the U.S. Capitol in Washington, D.C., will find these words by Captain Smith carved into the rotunda of the great building: "Pocahontas, the King's dearest daughter, when no entreaty would prevail, got his head in her arms, and laid her own upon his to save him from death."

This portrait of Captain John Smith hangs in the Library of Virginia. Born in England in 1579, Smith would find adventure away from his native country.

The Captain 2

John Smith was born January 2, 1579, in Lincolnshire, a rural county north of London near the North Sea. He was the son of George and Alice Smith, tenant farmers on the estate of a rich English lord. Although not a member of the **aristocracy**, whose members owned most of the land in the kingdom, George Smith was a man of some wealth, able to provide his family with a standard of living much higher than that of most of the other common people living in 16th-century England.

John Smith attended school, taking courses in English, Latin, Greek, and mathematics. At the age of 16, he left school with the intention of joining Queen Elizabeth's Royal Navy. However, his parents instead insisted that he learn a business. They sent him to the town of Lynn, where he *apprenticed* to Thomas Sendall, a rich merchant. It was a dull job. Young John Smith spent most of his workdays bent over a desk, keeping books and writing letters for Sendall.

He would spend just one year working for Sendall. In 1596, George Smith died, leaving John much of his small fortune. Smith took the money, left Sendall's employ, and made his way to Paris. Unlike dour London, Paris was an exciting, lively city full of parties and fun.

Smith quickly wasted his fortune. He spent some of his money on Paris's nightlife. He also gave money to people who promised they could help him gain a *prestigious* post with the Royal Highland Guards, the queen of England's personal bodyguards. The people who promised the appointment had no influence in the selection of the queen's guards. But they did know how to take money from unsuspecting young men far from home. When Smith realized he had been fooled, he was virtually penniless and too ashamed to return to Sendall. Instead, he volunteered for the French army.

He soon found himself a member of a French ***mercenary*** company. Mercenaries are soldiers who are hired to fight; they have no motive to defend a land or its people other than the money they are paid. Smith was issued a helmet and musket, and sent south to help find a Spanish ***cavalry*** regiment.

France had been enjoying an uneasy peace with Spain at the time; there were occasional skirmishes between the two nations, which share a common border along the Pyrenees Mountains. When Smith's company caught up with some Spanish cavalrymen, Smith had his first taste of combat. The Spaniards were quickly routed.

More skirmishes followed. Smith fought well and rose in rank to sergeant. But in 1597, Spain asked for peace. The war was over and so were jobs for the mercenaries. Smith was out of work, but not for long. Holland was fighting a long war to win its independence from Spanish rule, and it was in desperate need of mercenaries. Smith signed on and distinguished himself in that war as well; his name— albeit spelled "Smyt"—shows up in an account of a battle written by Maurice of Nassau, a Dutch general: "The paid horsemen . . . were inspired by the example of an English sergeant in the Duxbury company, one John Smyt, who laid about him with such rapid strokes that he left a path of Spanish dead in his wake."

Smith received a promotion to ensign. He also received a bullet wound that took six months to heal. By the time he was fit and ready for battle again, he was once again unemployed. In 1600, the Spanish retreated and the mercenaries were no longer needed. The Dutch paid them off and sent them home.

Smith spent a dull year in England, aching for more adventure. In time, he learned that the Central European states had launched an attack on the Turks. That meant there would once again be work for soldiers for hire.

Europeans had been fighting Turkey and other Islamic states for hundreds of years, dating back to the 11th century, when the first *Crusades* were fought. The Crusades were a series of wars Europeans waged against the Islamic states to win Jerusalem and other places of Christian religious importance away from Muslim rule. Mostly, the crusading armies failed. The Europeans managed to hold on to Jerusalem for less than 100 years. Meanwhile, thousands of Christian soldiers died in bloody battles that didn't cease until 1270, when a French army retreated after a battle against the Turks in North Africa.

Although the Crusades had been over for centuries, the Christian countries of Europe continued to make war against the Turks until the early 1600s. In time, this conflict would become known as the "Long War."

Smith was delighted to jump into the fight. And at this point in his life, Smith also decided to start writing down accounts of his exploits. Over the next few years, he would fill pages and pages with stories of mutinies, piracies, shipwrecks, and other adventures. On his way to the war, Smith claimed, he found work on a pirate ship, cruising the Mediterranean Sea in search of booty. In 1602, after two years of life aboard the ship, Smith landed in Naples, Italy. He then made his way to Vienna, Austria, with the intention of offering his services in the war against the Turks. He soon found work in the army of the Earl of Volda-Meldritch, a Hungarian nobleman, who hired him as a lieutenant.

And so John Smith, English-born and a veteran of the French and Dutch armies, was now fighting for Hungary.

This painting by Philips Wouwerman depicts a skirmish between Hungarian and Turkish troops. Smith served the Hungarian side well, and was soon promoted to captain.

The Hungarians marched into Transylvania, a region of high mountains that is now in present-day Romania. They had no trouble finding Turks; Meldritch's army engaged the enemy in fierce and bloody battles. Smith fought with distinction and was soon promoted to captain, a rank he would insist on using for the rest of his life.

But at a battle at the Oltu River, high in the Transylvanian Alps, Meldritch's troops were

ambushed by Turkish archers and musketeers, and the Hungarians were routed. Many of the soldiers died in the battle. Meldritch escaped, but Smith was taken prisoner. He was sold into slavery and entered the service of Timor, a rich Turk who took him to his home in Adrianople in Turkey, about 30 miles from the Turkish capital of Constantinople. Today, Constantinople is known as Istanbul.

Timor put Smith to work in his fields, but in 1604 the captain escaped and made his way north to Russia, where he found sanctuary in the city of Rostov. Helped by Baron Reshdinski, a Russian nobleman, Smith traveled back to Hungary, where he discovered the war against the Turks had ended. He soon met up again with Meldritch, who gave his captain gold in appreciation for his service in the war and his escape from the Turks.

With his pockets filled, and with many great stories to tell, Smith booked passage back to England. After a leisurely trip through Europe, Smith was aboard the Portuguese ship *Leonora* on October 4, 1605, as it sailed up the Thames River to London.

Smith had been gone four years. When he returned, he found London abuzz with stories of the New World.

Jamestown

English colonists arrive at Virginia's shores in 1607 on the ships Susan Constant, God Speed, *and* Discovery. *These settlers hoped to establish a permanent settlement in North America.*

3

I n 1603, Queen Elizabeth I died, leaving the throne of England in the hands of a relative, King James I. The new king was anxious for England to catch up with France and Spain in exploring and claiming the vast new territories in North America.

Spain had been sending explorers and **conquistadors** to the New World since the voyages of Columbus some 100 years earlier, and had extended its kingdom into South

With the death of Queen Elizabeth in 1603, King James VI of Scotland took the throne of England, becoming King James I. The new king actively encouraged explorers such as Henry Hudson, Walter Raleigh, and John Smith.

America and Mexico. France, meanwhile, had staked claims in Canada. England was lagging behind. Although England had been sending explorations to America, its efforts to establish settlements had so far failed.

So King James granted a ***charter*** to the Virginia Company of London, with the idea that it would raise money from private investors to finance expeditions and settlements in the New World. Its first goal was to establish a settlement in Virginia.

Stories of the Spanish conquistadors and their discoveries of gold in Peru and Mexico had long ago reached England, and the directors of the Virginia Company were certain such riches could be unearthed elsewhere in the New World. They proposed that the initial settlers land in Virginia, build a small fort, and make preparations to establish a much larger settlement. Eventually, the Company believed, thousands of English citizens would migrate to the New World, which would create a market for English goods outside the British Isles.

In addition, the Virginia Company's directors believed that the New World was actually quite small. They thought all that separated the Atlantic Ocean from the Pacific Ocean was a narrow strip of land. It would be the job of the settlers to map the region and find a route to the Pacific Ocean. Then the Company could send ships to Asia. There, valuable goods not available in Europe could be purchased and brought back to sell in England.

While the directors of the Virginia Company were busy designing these grand schemes, John Smith was making the rounds of English taverns, telling stories of his adventures. People wanted to meet this man who had led such an exciting life. One man eager to meet Smith was Sir Walter Raleigh. During the 1570s and 1580s, Raleigh had planned expeditions to America. By 1605, though, Raleigh was unable to continue his explorations–he had been locked up in the Tower of London by King James, who suspected him of **treason**.

Still, Raleigh sent word out that he wanted to meet John Smith. The captain agreed to meet the old explorer in his prison cell. Certainly, Smith did not need much prompting to relate his adventures to Raleigh, but during their meetings in the Tower Smith also found himself listening to Raleigh's stories of exploration and his descriptions of America.

Smith was intrigued with the idea of sailing to the New World. So when he learned that the Virginia Company was searching for investors, Smith contributed a large sum of money. He also decided to make the trip himself.

First, the company bought three ships: the *Susan Constant*, *God Speed*, and *Discovery*. Smith devoted himself to planning the voyage, buying supplies, and recruiting settlers. Eventually, Smith helped sign up 150 volunteers willing to make the voyage, including bricklayers, stone masons, carpenters, and other tradesmen. Also, quite a few soldiers signed up, two of whom were George Kendall, a former infantry captain, and Gabriel Archer, who had fought as a mercenary in Holland. Kendall and Archer would soon play important roles in Smith's life—they would become his bitter enemies.

In addition to tradesmen and military men, the expedition also found itself with a considerable number of "gentlemen," well-off men of London who were unaccustomed to physical labor or the harsh conditions of life in the wilderness. The Virginia Company's decision to permit such men to make the trip would prove to be a major blunder. Once in the New World, the settlers would discover that these men had few talents that would prove useful in establishing a settlement.

Another mistake committed by the Virginia Company was its failure to establish the colony's leaders before the ships sailed for America. Instead, the directors met in secret and drew up a charter for the new colony's government. The charter was locked in a box, with instructions that it couldn't be opened until the ships landed in the New World.

Only men were included in the first expedition of the Virginia Company. It was decided that men would establish the settlement, and women would cross the ocean and join them later.

But with no clear leaders for the voyage, the men aboard ship quickly found themselves involved in petty disputes. No one could settle disagreements.

The ships set sail down the Thames on January 1, 1607. Smith traveled aboard the *Susan Constant,* sharing quarters with Gabriel Archer. Aboard ship, he was his typical boastful, vain self, telling his war stories and acting as though he considered himself the leader. Archer, who considered *himself* the leader of the expedition, bristled at Smith's arrogance.

It was not an easy journey. Bad weather slowed the ships. Men grew sick and died from the rigors of the voyage. By the time land was sighted, 45 of the original 150 travelers had died.

The coat of arms of the Virginia Company of London. The company was established to help England compete with France and Spain for a share of the New World.

Smith had his own troubles. George Kendall had befriended Archer, and Smith now had two enemies. One day, an argument erupted. Smith said Kendall and Archer called him "names so foul that no man could tolerate such abuse." Smith responded by drawing his sword. Kendall and Archer backed down, but they persuaded others aboard the ship to hold a "court of inquiry" into the incident. The court tried Smith, found him guilty, and sentenced him to death! He was to be hanged as soon as the expedition reached land.

Smith laughed this off in his typical arrogant way, knowing full well that anyone who approached him with the idea of carrying out the court's sentence would have to fight, sword to sword. "I knew that there was no swordsman in that miserable lot who could stand up to me," the captain wrote.

The ships sailed south and by March had reached the islands of the Caribbean, where they stopped for supplies. With everyone enjoying themselves on the tropical beaches, tempers seemed to ease. No one gave much thought to hanging Smith. On April 10, the ships headed north again, but they ran into a storm. After they drifted for several days, many of the settlers wished to return to England.

Smith insisted they keep searching for land, though. He succeeded in changing enough minds, and the voyage continued. However, he was brash and pushy in his arguments and clashed again with Kendall and Archer.

The expedition sighted land on April 25. The ships entered a large mouth of water Smith would later name the Chesapeake Bay, anchoring off a shoreline the settlers called Cape Henry. Smith led a landing party ashore, and the men made camp in a grassy meadow surrounded by tall trees.

Their first night in America was not peaceful. As soon as they lit their campfire, they found themselves under attack by Native Americans. The members of the landing party quickly fired their muskets. The Indians had never heard or seen such weapons, and they scattered in fear upon hearing the blasts.

The next morning, back aboard ship, the settlers opened the box containing the colony's charter. The Virginia Company's directors had appointed a seven-member council to govern the settlement. Smith was named to the council. So was his enemy Kendall. The seven members would, in turn, elect a president of the colony. Disputes would be put to a vote, with majority rule.

*The English colonists, led by Captain Smith, row ashore
at Cape Henry, Virginia, in April 1607.*

The ships found a suitable place to anchor at the
mouth of what the settlers named the James River,
in honor of the king. For the next two weeks, Smith
led small expeditions up the James River, encountering friendly Indians and sharing their food. On
May 13, Smith guided the three ships up the James
River about 50 miles northwest of Cape Henry. The
expedition decided to settle in this area. Smith later
wrote that he had selected a "vcrie fit place for the
erecting of a great cittie." It would be called
Jamestown.

Exploring
Virginia

The English colonists set out to explore the new land, Virginia. Smith led several scouting expeditions, during which he made the first maps of the region and met the local Native Americans and their powerful chief, Powhatan.

4

Smith picked the site for Jamestown based on its military advantages. The settlers were unsure of the intentions of the Indians. After all, Smith and his small party had been attacked their first night ashore. Plus, the English settlers were fearful of the Spanish, who also had claims in the New World.

The location selected for the settlement had a deep-water mooring for the three ships, and it was far enough up the James River to be out of sight of passing Spanish warships. It was nearly an island, surrounded on three sides by the river and marshes.

"Heaven and Earth never agreed to better frame a place for man's habitations," declared Smith.

Well, maybe not. The settlers had elected to build the colony in a swamp. Around the settlement, water stood in marshy pools that attracted mosquitoes and other harmful insects. The settlers suffered from diseases like *malaria*, *typhus*, and *dysentery*. The first summer was blisteringly hot; the first winter bitterly cold. Of the 105 men who landed in Jamestown on May 13, 1607, only 38 would still be there six months later. Many would die from disease, the climate, or Indian attacks, while others would choose to return to England.

The London gentlemen who made the trip proved themselves virtually useless in Virginia. They knew nothing about how to build shelters or find food. They were lazy. The tradesmen who did work complained bitterly about them. Arguments were frequent.

Somehow, though, Jamestown managed to rise out of the swamp. The settlers built a wooden fort. Inside, they erected cabins and a church.

The English begin construction of their fort at Jamestown in 1607. Smith selected the location for strategic reasons.

Smith described their small church: "I well remember, we did hang an awning which is an old saile to three or four trees to shadow us from the Sunne, our walls were rales of wood, our seats unhewed trees till we cut plankes. In foul weather we shifted into an old rotten tent."

Smith began his first real exploration of the James River a few weeks after the settlers landed. The settlers built a small boat called a ***shallop***.

Christopher Newport, captain of the *Susan Constant,* commanded the shallop, but Smith went along to lead landing parties ashore to explore the Virginia forests. The shallop sailed about 70 miles up the James River, stopping along the way so that Smith and his landing party could scout the region.

Smith found himself making friends quite easily with the local Indians. He picked up bits and pieces of their language and was the only settler in those first few months who could communicate with them. Smith may have met Powhatan on this trip and presented the chief with gifts. During this first visit, Powhatan may have helped Smith draw one of the first maps of Virginia.

Captain Smith described Powhatan as "a tall well proportioned man, with a sower look, his head somewhat gray, his beard so thinne, that it seemeth none at all, his age neare sixtie, of a very able and hardy body to endure any labour."

Smith made other trips up the river in the shallop

If Captain Smith met Powhatan during this early exploration, it casts doubt on the story of his capture and near execution by Powhatan later in the year. Why would Powhatan order the death of somebody who had given him gifts?

that summer. He traded with the Native Americans, giving them axes and cooking pots in exchange for food. The Indians also showed Smith how to dry deerskin and buffalo hides and fashion them into shirts, trousers, and coats. When winter arrived, these garments proved to be warmer than any the settlers had brought with them from England.

During the winter, Smith continued to make his way up and down the James River, exploring the wilderness, drawing maps, and making friends with the Indians. It was on December 29, 1607, that Smith had his famous encounter with Powhatan and his supposed rescue by Pocahontas.

Only a few days later, disaster struck the settlement. On January 7, 1608, the cabins, church, and timber wall around the fort burned down when sparks from a fire lit the cabin roofs, which had been fashioned from thin wooden reeds. So the settlers started over, building everything again.

The next day, on January 8, 1608, 80 new settlers arrived aboard the *Susan Constant*, which had returned to England some months earlier. And on April 20, another 40 settlers sailed in aboard the *Phoenix*, a fourth ship that had been obtained by the Virginia Company.

The Jamestown colonists watch their homes burn on the night of January 7, 1608. The next day, a new group of colonists arrived to help rebuild the settlement.

Women were among the recent arrivals. Jamestown was no longer just a camp in the woods; it had become a bustling little community where people could settle down and raise families. Anne Burras arrived in 1608. Within three months of stepping off the boat, she wed carpenter John Laydon. It was the first marriage in Jamestown.

Although supply ships arrived with food and the tools and raw materials needed to build homes and start small farms, the settlers were often left to their own resourcefulness when it came to providing the other necessities of life. For example, the settlers learned how to make their own glass. They built a small factory near Jamestown and within six months were making glass to export to England. They grew *flax*–a plant used to make linen–and spun its fiber into thread. They slaughtered animals and tanned their hides into leather. They used the coarse red clay they found in the dirt around Jamestown to make their own pottery.

The settlers also had to deal with diseases, and for that they needed medicines. In Europe in the late 1500s, doctors had discovered the healing powers of herbs. The settlers brought many of these healing plants with them to Jamestown. However, the herbs eventually ran out, and the settlers had to scour the countryside for replacements. They discovered that certain tree barks were effective against malaria, that tobacco helped rid the body of worms, and that *ipecac* could treat some stomach ailments. In their gardens, the colonists grew such herbs as hyssop, lavender, comfrey, and fennel, all of which were found to have some medical uses.

Many of the new Jamestown colonists had spent considerable time in London's taverns before making the trip to the New World. There were, of course, no taverns in Jamestown, so the colonists learned how to brew their own beer. All of the ingredients were easily at hand: water was plentiful, and grain grew easily. The settlers usually used barley, but corn, oats, wheat, or rye would work as well. Finally, **hops**–part of a vine similar to a mulberry and used to flavor beer–could be found growing wild near the settlement.

On June 2, 1608, Smith took the shallop and led a group of 13 colonists down the James River to Cape Henry, then turned north and entered the Chesapeake Bay. They traveled slowly so Smith could make careful sketches of the shoreline. Along the way, the explorers encountered friendly Native Americans, who knew the territory and helped Smith fill in the details on the maps he drew of the Chesapeake. On June 16, Smith discovered the mouth of the Potomac River. It was an exciting discovery; the Potomac was obviously a major waterway. Nearly two centuries later, the capital of the young United States of America would be established along the Potomac's banks.

Smith and the explorers traveled about 30 miles up the Potomac. They met up with some hostile

The winter of 1607-8 was very hard for the English settlers. Many died from malnutrition and disease.

Indians but scared them off by firing muskets. They spent the next several days exploring and mapping the region and catching fish, but in early July one of the explorers, Anas Todkill, tripped over a rock and broke his leg. Smith decided it was time to return to Jamestown.

They arrived back at the settlement July 21, seven weeks after they had left to explore the Chesapeake and Potomac. Smith and his men found Jamestown in chaos.

The Colonists
Get to Work

Captain Smith (seated) bargains with a group of Native Americans. Unfortunately, the colonists' dealings with the Indians were not always so peaceful.

5

ohn Ratcliffe, captain of the *Discovery,* one of the original Virginia Company ships, was president of Jamestown in July 1608. A moody man who was prone to violent fits of anger, Ratcliffe had been unable to deal with Jamestown's growing list of ills during the seven weeks of Smith's absence. Many of the settlers unaccustomed to the sweltering Virginia summer were sick. Food was again scarce. Ratcliffe further infuriated the settlers when he ordered them to put down their work and build a house for him. Sensing that he would soon have a mutiny on his hands, Ratcliffe voluntarily stepped down as president.

When Smith's party returned from the Chesapeake, a group of settlers approached the captain and asked him to take over as president. At first, Smith refused. He thought Ratcliffe should resume his duties because it was important for the colonists to learn how to live under a government. He believed that the intended government should be honored. But the colonists persisted, and Smith finally agreed to step in.

His first act was to appoint settler Matthew Scrivener his chief deputy. He gave Scrivener the authority to act as president in his absence, an important appointment because Smith intended to leave the colony to search for food. In fact, three days after accepting the presidency, Smith took the shallop and nine colonists back to the Chesapeake Bay. He encountered some friendly Indians there, who gave him 400 large baskets of corn as well as a supply of deer meat to take back to Jamestown. Smith wrote that there were "so many bales of dried venison that the shallop sat low in the water."

Jamestown colonists load a ship with large barrels (called hogsheads) filled with dried tobacco leaves. Tobacco soon became one of the colony's most important exports.

Back at Jamestown, there was other work to do. Smith decided that what the colonists needed was a tough administrator, someone who would settle their quarrels with authority and make sure they did their fair share of work. Indeed, he made work a requirement for food.

According to one of the books Smith wrote later, he told the settlers: "You see now that power rests wholly in myself: you must obey this now for a law, that he that will not work shall not eat, for the labors

of thirty or forty industrious men shall not be con-
sumed to maintain 150 idle loiterers."

In the best of times, Smith was not the most
beloved man in Jamestown. Since arriving in the
New World the year before, Smith had continued to
be a boastful, vain man. He had few friends in
Jamestown, and his order that "he that will not work
shall not eat" won him new enemies among the
colony's lazy gentlemen.

Things soon got worse. Some of the settlers
planned to steal the shallop and sail up the coast to
Newfoundland, where they hoped to find passage
back to London aboard an English fishing vessel.
Smith sniffed out the plot and put an end to it. "If I
find any more runners for Newfoundland, let him
assuredly look to arrive at the gallows," Smith told
the colonists.

Other settlers who broke rules found themselves
imprisoned in Jamestown's *pillory*, a device in
which the offender's hands and head could be
locked. Lawbreakers sentenced to the pillory had to
stand in Jamestown's public square until Smith
ordered them released.

Indians who crossed Smith were treated no
better. While Smith often had good relations with

A pair of Indians pursue colonists who have strayed too far from the English fort. Relations between the Native Americans and the English grew worse as more settlers arrived in Virginia.

the Native Americans, he felt it wise to treat them harshly to establish his authority. Indians were often imprisoned, kept in chains, or forced into labor. Smith once personally administered 20 lashes with a rope to an Indian.

New settlers arrived in September 1608. They brought along a new charter from the Virginia

Company. Word of the colony's ills had made it back to England, and the directors of the Virginia Company decided it was time to change the manner of government in Jamestown. Smith was ousted and colonist Francis West was named the new president.

West's first problem was how to feed the newly arrived settlers. With winter approaching, West decided to take 120 settlers up the James River to establish a new colony. He thought that if the crops failed at Jamestown or game became scarce there, this second colony could provide another source of food. Smith went along with West's group to act as a scout and interpreter in case the settlers needed to speak with the Native Americans.

The Indians that lived in the area where West wanted to settle proved to be hostile. Two settlers were killed by Indians when they strayed too far from the camp. The nervous men soon built a fort.

The site where Francis West's party made camp would eventually become the city of Richmond. Today, this city is the capital of the state of Virginia.

Meanwhile, Smith met with the Indians and struck a deal to obtain land for the new settlement. He believed the site where West wanted to settle was too prone to flooding. West turned down the deal, though. This caused a heated argument between the two men.

Because West and Smith could not get along, Smith decided to return to Jamestown. With five loyal men, Smith left in one of the group's small boats. They made their way down the James River.

One night, while the men were sleeping in the boat, a spark ignited a gunpowder pouch that Smith wore around his waist. Smith suddenly awoke to find himself on fire. He suffered severe burns and nearly drowned when he jumped in the river to douse the flames. His men carried him back to Jamestown. There, however, Smith believed his old enemy Gabriel Archer planned to have him murdered.

Stripped of the presidency of Jamestown, badly burned by the accident in the boat, and now fearing that his life was in danger, Smith decided it was time to return to England.

A statue of John Smith overlooks the James River in Virginia. After leaving Jamestown in 1608, Smith never returned to the colony. However, he did continue exploring, mapping the coast of New England in 1614.

Exploring New England

6

espite continuing difficulties, the Jamestown settlement would go on to make its mark in American history. It became the first self-governing colony in America. In 1619, the Virginia Company, hoping to improve conditions in the colony, permitted the residents to establish a General Assembly, made up of representatives who were freely elected.

Tobacco, which soon became an important cash crop in the American colonies, was first grown in Jamestown by John Rolfe. Rolfe was also the husband of Pocahontas. After their marriage, Rolfe took her to England, where the young Indian princess died of disease in 1617. It is believed she succumbed to either influenza, pneumonia, or smallpox, illnesses that doctors were unable to treat effectively in the 17th century.

Jamestown was in some ways responsible for the sparks that would ignite two of America's wars. The English government did not allow tobacco growers to sell their crops to other countries. All such sales had to be made through brokers in London, where heavy taxes were levied. The tobacco growers did not like the law, which cut deeply into their profits. Later, other exporters in America would also oppose such treatment at the hands of the British government. This issue of taxation without representation would be one of the causes of the American Revolution in 1776.

The other war that can be directly traced to Jamestown is the American Civil War, fought in large part to free the slaves of the South. In 1619, 20 Africans were brought to Jamestown to work in the tobacco fields. They were the first Africans forced to work in the New World. By the outbreak of the Civil War in 1861, nearly four million African slaves would be in bondage in the Southern states.

꿈ꦸꦸꦸ

After leaving Jamestown in 1608, Captain John Smith never returned. However, he had already carved for himself a place in American history based on his accomplishments. Smith had helped finance and organize the expedition, and during his nearly two years in Virginia he served as a leader in Jamestown. He had also led most of the major explorations along the James River and the Chesapeake Bay.

But the captain was not one to sit still. Soon the promise of new adventures lured him back to the New World. In 1614, he embarked on a mission to explore territory well up the coast from Virginia. Smith named this region New England.

England had already sent a handful of missions to that area. In 1602 Captain Bartholomew Gosnold, who later commanded the *God Speed* on its voyage to Jamestown, had landed on Cape Cod in what is now Massachusetts. Other voyages followed, but by 1613 England was still looking for a toehold in this part of the New World.

Smith became a promoter of the idea. He was able to interest investors in financing a voyage of discovery by promising to hunt whales and large deep-sea fish while making the Atlantic crossing.

Whale oil had great commercial value in England. So did **ambergris**, a secretion of the whale's intestine used to make perfume.

Smith obtained two ships for the voyage, the *Queen Anne* and the *Frances*. They set sail for the New World on March 3, 1614. The expedition reached Canada in April, sailing past Newfoundland and Nova Scotia. From Nova Scotia, the ships sailed slowly down the coast. Smith drew maps of the shoreline, charting the coastal regions of Maine, New Hampshire, Massachusetts, and Rhode Island.

The crews found the fishing excellent, catching mostly cod and tuna. Smith estimated that the two ships caught some 50,000 fish in their trip down the American coast. After drying and salting the fish to preserve them, they stored the catch in the holds of the vessels.

Whales proved more elusive, however. The whales' skins were too tough for the harpoons Smith had brought. The animals also proved to be much faster and smarter than the men had anticipated, easily evading the fishing boats as they approached. In later years, whalers would refine and improve their hunting techniques, and New England would become an important whaling center.

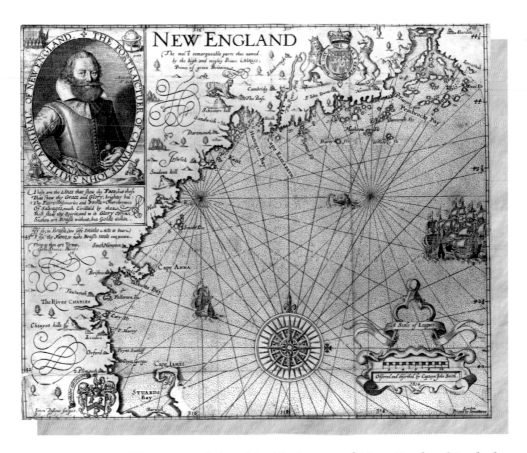

This copy of Smith's 1614 map of New England includes an engraving of the explorer and a poem about him.

In New Hampshire, Smith went ashore, encountering friendly Indians and trading with them. In Massachusetts, Smith explored the Merrimack River. Later, he spent two days on the future site of the city of Boston. He named a nearby river the Charles River, in honor of the son of King James.

In Rhode Island, Smith entered Narragansett Bay and made friends with the local Indians. By

THE
TRUE TRAVELS,
ADVENTVRES,
AND
OBSERVATIONS
OF
Captaine IOHN SMITH,
In *Europe*, *Asia*, *Affrica*, and *America*; from *Anno Domini* 1593. to 1629.

His Accidents and Sea-fights in the Straights; his Service
and Stratagems of warre in *Hungaria*, *Tranfilvania*, *Wallachia*, and
Moldavia, against the *Turks*, and *Tartars*; his three single combats
betwixt the *Chriftian* Armie and the *Turkes*.

After how he was taken prifoner by the *Turks*, fold for a Slave, fent into
Tartaria; his defcription of the *Tartars*, their ftrange manners and cuftomes of
Religions, Diets, Buildings, Warres, Feafts, Ceremonies, and
Living; how hee flew the Bafhaw of *Nalbrits* in *Cambia*,
and efcaped from the *Turkes* and *Tartars*.

Together with a continuation of his generall Hiftory of *Virginia*,
Summer-Iles, *New England*, and their proceedings, fince 1624. to this
prefent 1629; as alfo of the new Plantations of the great
River of the *Amazons*, the Iles of S.*Chriftopher*, *Mevis*,
and *Barbados* in the *Weft Indies*.

All written by actuall Authours, whofe names
you fhall finde along the Hiftory.

LONDON,
Printed by *F. H.* for *Thomas Slater*, and are to bee
fold at the Blew Bible in *Greene Arbour*. 1630.

This is the title page of one of John Smith's many books. These works made him famous and encouraged others to settle in North America.

then, summer had arrived. The mission had been planned to last just a few months, so Smith reluctantly agreed to turn back. The two ships set sail for England on July 18, arriving back in port in late August.

By now, Smith and his investors realized that the true riches of the New World had nothing to do with gold or jewels or even a water passage to the Pacific Ocean. Numerous attempts by Smith and others to find that passage in Virginia had failed. Instead, the English realized that the real treasures in the New World were the animals that could be trapped for their furs or the fish and whales that could be snared. It seemed as though these resources could provide an endless supply of food and oil that could be sold back in London and other European cities. What's more, America's vast forests could be harvested for lumber that could be shipped back to Europe. And eventually the trade would work both ways. With thousands of colonists expected to make their homes in the New World, the tools and provisions necessary to build their communities would have to be sold to them.

Smith wanted to return to the New World after completing his mission to New England, but he never got a chance. In 1620, the Pilgrims briefly considered hiring him to lead their expedition to Plymouth, but his independent nature and brash personality worried them. They hired Captain Miles Standish instead.

Captain John Smith died on June 21, 1631, at the age of 52. He spent his last years telling others to sail to the New World. He wrote several books about his voyages, hoping to persuade his readers that they, too, could find adventure in North America. "I have drawn a map from point to point, isle to isle and harbor to harbor, with the soundings, sands, rocks, and landmarks I passed close aboard the shore in a little boat," Smith wrote. "I had not the power to search as I would. Thus you may see, of this two thousand miles of New World coastal lands, more than half is unknown to any purpose."

Chronology

1579 John Smith is born on January 2 in Lincolnshire, England.

1596 Arrives in Paris and joins a company of mercenaries fighting in the French army.

1602 Joins the Hungarian army as a mercenary in a war against Turkey. Promoted to captain. Captured in battle and sold into slavery.

1603 King James I takes the throne in England. The new king encourages English exploration of the New World.

1604 Smith escapes and makes his way back to England, arriving October 4, 1605.

1605 Meets Sir Walter Raleigh in the Tower of London. The old explorer encourages Smith to travel to the New World.

1607 On January 1, sets sail for Virginia as member of a 150-man expedition on the ships *Susan Constant, God Speed*, and *Discovery*; on April 25, the ships arrive in Virginia, anchoring in the Chesapeake Bay. Smith leads a small party ashore; on May 13, the ships sail up the James River and anchor at the site of the new settlement, to be called Jamestown; while exploring the James River, Smith meets the Indian chief Powhatan on December 29. He later claims that during this episode his life is saved by Powhatan's daughter, Pocahontas.

1608 Much of Jamestown burns down when a spark ignites the roofs of the cabins on January 7. A day later, 80 new settlers arrive in Jamestown, followed by 40 more on April 20; the new settlers include the first female colonists. On

June 2, Smith begins an exploration of Virginia that includes the discovery of the Potomac River; in July, Smith is named president of Jamestown and given the job of restoring order to the troubled colony. Issues order that "he that will not work shall not eat." In September, Smith is relieved of Jamestown's presidency; after he is burned in a gunpowder accident, Smith returns to England.

1614 Leads an expedition to New England, mapping parts of Maine, New Hampshire, Massachusetts, and Rhode Island.

1617 Pocahontas dies in England.

1619 The first popularly elected General Assembly in America convenes in Jamestown. The first Africans arrive at the colony and are put to work in the tobacco fields.

1631 John Smith dies in England on June 21.

Glossary

ambergris–a waxy substance from the intestine of the sperm whale that is used to make perfume.

ambush–a trap in which soldiers hide themselves, so as to attack by surprise.

apprentice–to work for a person skilled in a trade or craft in exchange for learning from that person.

aristocracy–the wealthy members of the ruling class.

cavalry–soldiers who fight while mounted on horses.

charter–written instructions and rules that detail how a city, state, or other institution should be governed.

conquistadors–soldiers leading Spain's conquest of Mexico, Peru, and parts of North America in the 16th century.

Crusades–a series of military operation undertaken by Christian nations of Europe during the 11th, 12th, and 13th centuries, with the intent of capturing the Holy Land from the Muslims.

dysentery–a disease, usually caused by infection, in which patients lose blood and have severe diarrhea.

expedition–a journey made by a group of people for a specific purpose, such as exploration or conquest; also, the group of people making the journey.

flax–a plant whose fiber is used to make linen.

hops–mulberry-like berries used to give beer its bitter flavor.

initiation–the process of becoming a member of a group or society.

ipecac–a substance found in certain plants that is used to treat stomach problems and poisoning.

malaria–a disease of the blood, transmitted by mosquitoes, that causes severe chills and fever and can be deadly.

mercenary–a soldier hired by a foreign country who works only for money.

millstone–a flat rock used to grind corn, wheat, and other crops into grain.

musket–a heavy muzzle-loading weapon that fires a large-caliber ball or projectile.

pillory–a wooden frame used to punish lawbreakers, containing three holes in which the offender's hands and head can be locked.

prestigious–honored or respected by most people.

shallop–a small open boat that can be rowed or sailed in shallow water.

skirmish–a brief or minor fight in a larger conflict.

treason–the crime of betraying or attempting to overthrow a leader to whom a person owes allegiance.

typhus–a severe bacterial disease that causes high fever, delerium, intense headaches, and a dark red rash.

Further Reading

Bridenbaugh, Carl. *Jamestown 1544-1699*. New York: Oxford University Press, 1980.

Chippendale, Neil. *Sir Walter Raleigh and the Search for El Dorado*. Philadelphia: Chelsea House Publishers, 2002.

Gerson, Noel B. *The Glorious Scoundrel: A Biography of Captain John Smith*. New York: Dodd, Mead and Company, 1978.

Hume, Ivor Noel. *The Virginia Adventure*. New York: Alfred A. Knopf, 1994.

Knight, James E. *Jamestown: A New World Adventure*. Mahwah, N.J.: Troll Press, 1998.

Mello, Tara Baukus. *John Smith: English Explorer and Colonist*. Philadelphia: Chelsea House Publishers, 2000.

Saffer, Barbara. *Henry Hudson: Ill-Fated Explorer of North America's Coast*. Philadelphia: Chelsea House Publishers, 2002.

Sakurai, Gail. *The Jamestown Colony*. New York: Children's Press, 1997.

Index

Picture Credits

HAL MARCOVITZ is a reporter for the *Allentown (Pa.) Morning Call.* His other book for Chelsea House include biographies of explorers John C. Frémont, Marco Polo, Francisco Vasquez de Coronado; the Indian guide Sacagawea; and the Apollo astronauts. He lives in Chalfont, Pennsylvania, with his wife, Gail, and daughters, Ashley and Michelle.